GO FOR IT!

AF378790

Calling all humanoids!

I'm Lektron the robot and I'd like to welcome you to *Go For It!* In this people-packed issue of *The Navigator*, you'll find out about some interesting human beings who have done some pretty amazing things. Take Archimedes, the Greek scientist who made rather a big splash with his discoveries. You'll also follow Nelson Mandela on his journey from prisoner to president of South Africa. You can also find out TV chef Jamie Oliver's recipe for success. Maybe you'll be inspired to make some fantastic food or 'pukka tucker'!

Robots are pretty cool too!

Text Type	Literacy Skills	Wider Curriculum Links
Recount/ Autobiography	Skimming; making comparisons; deductive comprehension; expressing and justifying opinions	**Science** Unit 5A: Keeping healthy
Report	Information retrieval; summarising information; interpreting visual information	**Science** Unit 5A: Keeping healthy
Report	Summarising content; language analysis	**Design and Technology** 5A: Musical instruments
Report/ Recount	Expressing and justifying opinions; information retrieval; summarising information; close reading	**Geography** Unit 11: Water
Report/ Recount	Information retrieval; inferential comprehension; expressing and justifying opinions	**History** Unit 13: How has life in Britain changed since 1948?
Report/ Recount	Information retrieval; inferential comprehension; expressing and justifying opinions	**History** Unit 13: How has life in Britain changed since 1948?
Recount/ Report/ Instructional	Asking questions	**Design and Technology** Unit 5D: Biscuits
Recount (visual)	Summarising information	**History** Unit 15: How do we use Greeks ideas today?
Persuasive/ Discussion	Identifying fact and opinion; expressing and justifying opinions; comparing information	**PSHE:** Preparing to play an active role as citizens
Recount	Information retrieval; expressing and justifying opinions	
Fun spread		
		ICT: Year 5 Schemes of work

WHAM-BAM

A website message from your wrestling hero

Hi fans! Welcome to my terrific website. Here's the story of my incredible life.

My real name is Simon Smithers, and I loved wrestling from a very early age. While other kids were watching Postman Pat on TV, I was tuning into wrestling programmes. When I was eight, I joined a kickboxing club in Hitchin, and shortly after became interested in karate and other martial arts. At eleven, I sent for a mail-order study pack on how to become a professional wrestler. I used to practise in the bathroom. Let me tell you, fans, the loofah and the toilet brush didn't stand a chance!

By the time I left school, wrestling was all I could think about. I only developed an interest in girls when I saw Suzie Meat and Dawn Draco slogging it out at the Hitchin Arena. Suzie lost that fight but she won my heart, and we were married on my 18th birthday.

No one could beat me at wrestling back then. I won hundreds of titles, including the ITV6 Super Ring Challenge Cup – probably my proudest moment, along with the birth of my kids, Biff and Tussle.

The rest is history. Some say that I'm history too, but that's just sour grapes. I'm 29 now, and the best performances are yet to come.

Keep on rooting for the old Wham-Bam, fans!

SOCKOWSKI

Me again, fans! Check out this article by Maurice Tomkins which appeared in the *Hitchin Express Sports Supplement*, on April 4 2002

THE HANDS OF THE GENTLE GIANT

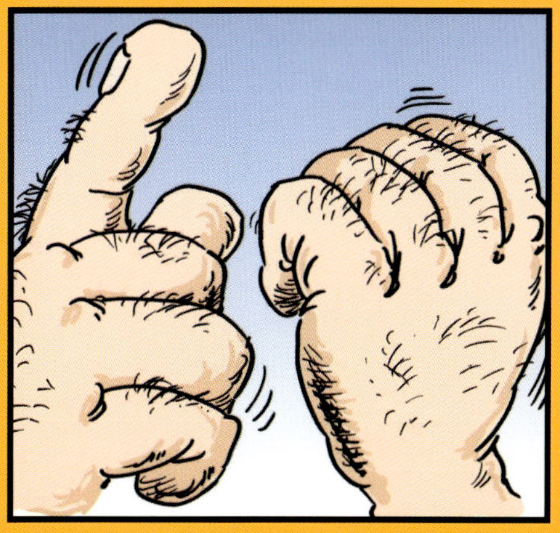

My statistics

Height: 2 metres (give or take a centimetre)

Weight: 227 lbs (don't ask me what that is in kilos)

Birthplace: Hitchin, Hertfordshire

Father's profession: Postman

Mother's profession: Fork-Lift Truck Driver

Wrestling titles held: ITV6 Super Ring Challenge Cup, Hitchin and District Wrestler of the Month Medal

Wrestling aliases: Bambo, The Thudder, Super Sockowski

Despite their appearance, Wham-Bam's 'Killer Grippers' are not always as deadly as they seem…

Wham-Bam Sockowski, Hitchin's favourite wrestler, is famous for his huge hands, known as 'The Wham-Bam Killer Grippers'. Some say they've become so big from years of wrapping themselves around his opponents' faces.

But when I met Wham-Bam last week and shook one of the Grippers, it didn't crush my poor ordinary-sized hand as I had expected. His handshake was the softest, gentlest shake I've ever experienced! This isn't so strange after all, for he is also a kind and caring family man. The famous 'Killer Grippers' are the very same hands that tuck his two young children in at night…

The history of wrestling in Britain

Wrestling is a much older activity than most people realise. We all know that it was a competitive sport in the Olympic Games of Ancient Greece. But it was enjoyed as a sport much earlier than that. Wrestlers were depicted as far back as 3000 BC, on the murals of Egyptian tombs.

The Romans introduced a disciplined version of the sport to Britain, but there is evidence that the Celts had their own (less disciplined!) style before the Romans came. Over the centuries, a number of wrestling styles developed in different parts of the country. One, known as Cumberland and Westmorland style, is thought to have been brought over by the Vikings.

Wrestling was a regular activity in Britain right into Victorian times, and a very popular spectator sport. Public interest began to fall off with the introduction of so-called Greco-Roman wrestling. In Greco-Roman wrestling, no holds were allowed below the waist, so combatants could spend a great deal of time fighting on the floor. As a bout could last for several hours, this could make for pretty boring viewing!

WRESTLING FACTS

1 So seriously did the people of Cornwall take the sport that in the Hundred Years War the Cornish banner showed two entwined wrestlers.

2 Wrestling on the village green had become a common sport by the end of the 19th century. All the men who wanted to fight, threw their caps into the air at the same time. Caps that fell next to one another resulted in their owners being matched to fight – regardless of weight, age or size!

3 The different wrestling styles traditionally used in places like Cornwall, Devon, Lancashire, and Cumberland and Westmorland are rarely seen these days. The wrestling we see on TV is more often than not based on Japanese and Eastern European styles.

A FAMOUS WRESTLING PUB

You've heard the old song, Pop Goes the Weasel?

Up and down the City Road,
In and out of The Eagle,
That's the way the money goes,
Pop goes the Weasel.

Well, The Eagle Tavern is a real pub in London. But there was a time when it was famous for something other than its alcohol. In the 1820s, regular wrestling matches were held there. Wrestlers from all over the country would come to The Eagle to fight. Spectators would place bets on who would win the fights – and often lose their money. 'That's the way the money goes … '

STOMP

making music on a dustbin

Can you make music with dustbin lids and broom handles? Or with plastic containers? You can, because that is just what Stomp does. What is Stomp? It's a band started in 1991 by Steve McNicholas and Luke Cresswell.

A Stomp show does not have any words and the music does not have melody, like music from a piano or a guitar. A Stomp show is all about dance and rhythm.

Luke Cresswell, who comes from Brighton, taught himself to be a percussionist – someone who plays instruments such as drums, tambourines and cymbals. Luke first started to improvise by drumming on objects around him, like bicycles and lamposts. He says you can make music out of absolutely anything, "tapping an old Coke can, or picking up pebbles on a beach. People are using rhythm all the time, even when they drum their fingers on a table or tap their feet because they are impatient or bored."

Luke met Yorkshireman Steve McNicholas in 1981, when his band joined forces with the theatre company Steve was in. Luke and Steve started to experiment using dustbins as drums after seeing the Burundi drummers from Africa. Then they began working on more acts, using different everyday items as their instruments.

The acts have a theme – they are not just about eight people drumming. The performers have to dance and they have to drum. After that, the ideas for the show grow in different ways. Sometimes an act is a visual idea – how it looks is as important as how it sounds. Other acts are purely about rhythm.

The instruments Stomp uses are
all everyday utensils, including
dustbin lids – which are used
like cymbals – dustbins, buckets,
brooms, plastic containers –
which make good bass drums –
sinks and draining boards.
One act involves performers
walking on oil drums with ski
boots fitted to them.

Today, Stomp has five companies:
two in the United Kingdom and
three in North America. These
companies perform all over the
world. Each company has twelve
performers, although only eight
are ever on stage at one time.
The shows have such energy and
tempo that the performers need a
rest every now and then!

And why did they choose the word
'Stomp'? Quite simply, Steve and
Luke just liked the image the name
conjured up. They think it describes
their kind of performance. "It's not
tap dance and it's not Wellington-
boot dance, or clog dance, it's

STOMPING."

Imagine living in a tube underwater for days on end. Or throwing yourself into the sea with your feet in a bucket of cement. These are just some of the jobs people do when they work in water!

Water World

Stunt diver

Christina Fetters works as a stunt diver in adventure films. She began her career scuba-diving as a stand-in for an actress in a film. Christina then went on to do scenes involving high falls and stunt diving. Her jobs have included swimming in milk, being thrown off a cliff with her feet in a bucket of cement, and coming within centimetres of a spinning propeller in icy water.

Christina Fetters

Underwater cameraman

Wildlife cameraman Doug Allan has filmed underwater sequences that had never been seen before, such as killer whales hunting grey whales, and polar bears hunting beluga whales. Doug worked for the British Antarctic Survey for ten years as a marine biologist, diver and base commander before becoming a wildlife cameraman for the BBC. He has worked on programmes such as *The Blue Planet* and *Life in the Freezer*.

Doug Allan

Undersea explorer

Robert Ballard has led over a hundred deep sea expeditions, using manned and unmanned vehicles. His discoveries include the German battleship *Bismarck* and, most famously, the *Titanic*. He also set up the Jason Project, to enable school children to follow his progress on undersea explorations around the globe. His current project is in the Black Sea, looking for evidence of a great flood that may have inspired the story of Noah's Ark.

Robert Ballard

Linda Greenlaw

Swordfisher

Linda Greenlaw is the only woman to captain a swordfishing boat. She has been fishing for over twenty years, and works in the waters east of Newfoundland. Linda began working as a cook and deckhand on board a swordfishing boat in summer breaks from college. She became a captain in 1986, and since then has caught swordfish in waters from Newfoundland to Brazil.

Did you know?

The Aquarius Project is the world's only underwater habitat, where scientists research the world's oceans. It is located twenty metres under the sea at Conch Reef, just off the coast of Florida, USA. Aquarius is a fifteen-metre-long cylinder, measuring just three metres in diameter, attached to the sea floor. It can hold six aquanauts, who stay on board for ten-day missions. They eat and sleep underwater, spending up to nine hours a day on diving missions.

Aquanaut Mark Hulsbeck checking the outside of the Aquarius cylinder. Mark has completed three missions on Aquarius.

Six of the best

In 2001, a panel of top British journalists took part in an interesting project. They had to select the 100 best performances by British sports stars between 1900 and 2000. Fifty of the performances in their final list took place in the half-century after 1950. During these five decades, Britain changed greatly. As the population soared and grew more racially mixed, people's lives were transformed by new technologies, new kinds of jobs, and new ways to enjoy increasing amounts of leisure time. More and more men, women and children took up sport for fun. They also became passionate 'armchair fans' of their nation's top sporting achievers – like these six from the journalists' list.

Roger Bannister (1954)

Before 1954, no athlete had ever run a mile in less than four minutes. Some experts believed it was impossible without doing terrible damage to the body. Then, on a blustery day in May at Oxford University's Iffley Road sports ground, medical student Roger Bannister proved them wrong. After months of careful training, he broke the 'four-minute barrier' by winning his race in 3 minutes 59.4 seconds. Although today's super-fit professional athletes can easily outstrip Bannister's time, his trail-blazing success is still acclaimed all over the world.

Geoff Hurst (1966)

No England football team played in the World Cup until 1950. As the inventors of modern football, the English assumed that they must be the best in the world at playing it. But in their first four World Cups, they did not even reach the semi-finals. Then at last, in July 1966, they made it to the final at London's Wembley Stadium. There they played West Germany for the right to be called World Champions. After extra time, the home team won by four goals to two – and England striker Geoff Hurst wrote himself into the record books as the first (and still the only) player to score three times in a World Cup final.

Virginia Wade (1977)

In the decades after World War II, women's sport became more competitive, skilful and popular. Only a few British sportswomen excelled at the highest level – and tennis star Virginia Wade was one of them. In July 1977, after fifteen previous attempts, she won the Wimbledon Championships by beating Holland's Betty Stove in the final. Her success in front of her home crowd – which included Queen Elizabeth II – was well-timed. Not only was this Wimbledon's centenary year, but Britain was also celebrating the Queen's Silver Jubilee.

Ian Botham (1981)

Many cricketers before 1950 came from privileged families. In later decades, good players from all parts of society got a fairer chance. Ian Botham had an 'ordinary' background, but from an early age he showed quite extraordinary talent. The scorer of 5200 runs for England and the taker of 383 wickets, his finest moment came in the Ashes Test series of 1981. With England facing almost certain defeat by Australia in the match at Headingly in Leeds, Botham scored 149 not-out to inspire one of England's most amazing victories.

Denise Lewis (2000)

Before the 2000 Olympic Games in Sydney, Australia, only five British female athletes had ever won gold medals. Denise Lewis added a sixth by winning the heptathlon, despite suffering an injury to her ankle. Lewis grew up in the West Midlands in a single-parent immigrant family, and had to show huge determination to achieve her success. In 2001, on receiving an OBE from Prince Charles, she pointed this out. "I reminded him how bad the facilities were," she said, "and he nodded and said it was true."

Steve Redgrave (1984, 1988, 1992, 1996, 2000)

At the age of forty, champion rower Steve Redgrave became an all-time great. At the 2000 Olympic Games he became the only athlete in history to win gold medals at five consecutive Olympics. His success at the highest level over a period of almost twenty years was astounding. This would not have been possible for an athlete in the past – because in addition to training hard and living healthily, Steve Redgrave depended on modern medication to combat his diabetes.

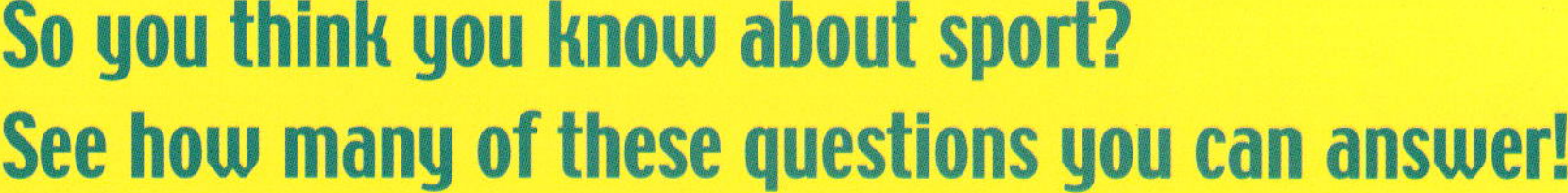

So you think you know about sport?
See how many of these questions you can answer!

1. Which British athlete won the Olympic decathlon twice?

2. Who was the oldest sprinter to win the Olympic 100 metres final?

3. To which British footballer did Pele say in 1970, "You are the greatest"?

4. Which ice dancing duo won gold at the 1984 Winter Olympics, with nine maximum scores for 'perfect and flawless performances'?

Answers 1. Daley Thompson, in 1980 and 1984 2. Britain's Linford Christie (aged 32), in 1992 3. England captain Bobby Moore 4. Jayne Torvill and Christopher Dean

Jamie Oliver was working in a restaurant kitchen when he was spotted by a TV producer. She liked his fresh face and breezy personality, and stuck him in front of a camera. He quickly shot to stardom and has produced three TV series and best-selling books. But what made Jamie tick as a child? Read on to find out more …

Meet
Jamie Oliver…

Child at work

Jamie was brought up in a busy pub-restaurant, run by his mum and dad. From the age of six, he liked to help out in the kitchen, peeling potatoes and shelling peas. "I grew up with seven chefs, using local ingredients, and cooking food became natural to me. It's just like breathing, really."

Favourite foods

Young Jamie loved 'pukka tucker' from the start and was always trying different things. As well as porridge, egg and bacon and liver sausage, he loved smoked salmon with lemon juice, and trout with salad. But most of all, Jamie loved Sunday roast dinners, sitting round the table laughing and talking with his mum, dad and sister, and any visiting aunts, uncles, cousins and grandparents.

Jamie's life story

Born: Clavering, Essex, in 1975.

Family: Son of Trevor and Sally, publicans of the Cricketer's Arms in Clavering.

Married: Childhood sweetheart, Juliette ('Jools') Norton in June 2000.

Education: Left school with a handful of GCSEs. At 16, went to Westminster Catering College, in London; spent a year cooking in France and Italy, then worked at the Neal Street Restaurant and River Café in London.

Television: First series of *'The Naked Chef'* screened in 1999; second in 2000; third in 2001.

Books: *'The Naked Chef'*, *'The Return of the Naked Chef'*, *'Happy Days with the Naked Chef'*. All bestsellers in over 30 countries.

Hobbies: Plays drums with his school mates in a band called Scarlet Division; supports Cambridge United; drives a Vespa.

Most memorable moment: Being invited to 10 Downing Street to prepare lunch for the British and Italian Prime Ministers.

Why not try one of Jamie's scrummy recipes?

Cooking for kids

Jamie wants to interest children and young people in food.

"Recently, me and six kids cooked this load of tucker and did a fantastic job of it and had a right good laugh at the same time." The secret lies in making delicious recipes like Banana and Honey Smoothies.

"I did this for my cousins for a treat. I also added a little peanut butter – mad! – but they liked it."

Banana and honey smoothie

For 2 people
2 bananas
3 tablespoons honey
approx 1 pint glass of ice
285 ml / ½ pint single cream

Place the bananas into a liquidiser and whizz for 30 seconds. Add the ice, honey and cream. Place the lid back on tightly and whizz up to a semi-slushy milkshake consistency.

EUREKA!

Archimedes was a Greek inventor and thinker who lived more than 2000 years ago.

Archimedes was very clever and loved finding things out, such as how levers worked.

One day, King Hiero came to see him. He was wearing a brand new crown.

The King wanted to know whether the goldsmith had replaced some gold with a cheaper, lighter metal like silver.

Archimedes weighed the crown against two gold bars and the scales balanced.

7

That night, when Archimedes was sitting in the tub, water overflowed onto the floor.

8

9

Archimedes was so excited, he ran straight to the King.

10

Archimedes knew that if the goldsmith had used the two gold bars, the crown would push up the same amount of water.

11

12

The King asked Archimedes to invent a machine that would punish the dishonest goldsmith.

Giving us goosebumps

American author R L Stine is an incredibly popular writer with boys and girls all over the world. As the title of his famous series *Goosebumps* suggests, Stine's books can be a bit scary! But there is plenty of humour in them too.

Here are some book reviews written by children:

One of my favourite 'Goosebumps' is 'Bride of the Living Dummy', sequel to 'Night of the Living Dummy'. This time Slappy (the dummy) wants real revenge on Eddie, but the plot gets very twisted. I think it's a carefully written book – every detail counts.
Sarah, 12

I think that 'The Ghost Next Door' is 'G' for GREAT!
This book is full of surprises and anyone who reads it will love it!

Alice, 10

'The Haunted School' is a brilliant book. It's about a boy called Tommy, who starts a new school and finds a lift that no one uses. It takes him to a place where everything is grey. The book is full of fun and excitement.

Leroy, 10

'The Girl Who cried Monster' is about a girl called Lucy who loves telling monster stories. One day she sees a librarian turn into a monster. This book has a really shocking ending. I loved this book and give it eleven out of ten.

Ben, 11

R L Stine has gone from writing joke books to becoming a master of horror

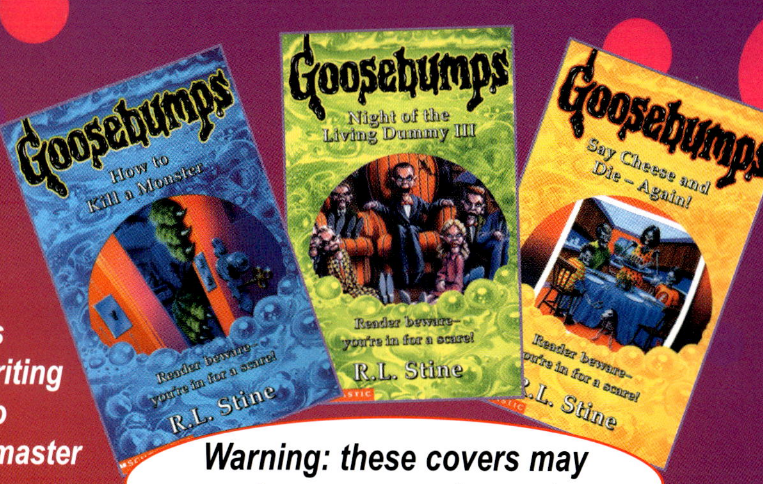

Warning: these covers may give you goosebumps!

Although many children enjoy Stine's books, adults are not always so enthusiastic about them. Some parents in America have campaigned to have the *Goosebumps* series removed from their children's school libraries because they think that the books are too scary for children. They also argue that Stine's books are not very well written and have no educational value.

These books do nothing to edify our children, or to promote decent morals, or kindness to one another.

Parent from Lynn Haven, Florida

There is enough violence in our society. We do not need to offer even more in our school libraries.

Parent from Coon Rapids, Minnesota

A lot of kids are very afraid of these books. They carry them around in their book bags and are afraid to read them.
Parent from Anoka-Hennepin, Minnesota

Nelson Mandela:

When Nelson Mandela was born on July 18 1918, in the tiny village of Mvezo in South Africa, little did his parents know that he would play such a great part in changing his country's history.

Hard times

When Mandela was growing up, black people in South Africa were not treated as equals to white people. Most black South Africans did not receive a good education, and were not given a say in how their country was run. Mandela wanted to do something to help these people.

The city calls

When he was 22, Mandela moved to Johannesburg, where he studied law. There he became a member of the African National Congress (ANC), a political group that worked to improve conditions for black South Africans.

Blacks and whites divided

In 1948, the South African government introduced a set of laws called apartheid, which made life even harder for black South Africans. They were forbidden to do certain jobs, they were not allowed to marry white people, and black children had to go to different schools from white children.

A life behind bars

In 1963, the police accused Mandela and some other ANC members of planning violent attacks against the government. Though he pleaded 'not guilty', Mandela was sentenced to spend the rest of his life in prison. Life there was extremely hard and he was not allowed to see his family.

Hard times: Mandela in prison

Time line

1918 Born on 18 July

1958 Marries Winnie Madikizela

1942 Joins ANC

1964 Sentenced to life imprisonment

1948 Apartheid laws introduced

from prisoner to president

The 'Free Mandela' campaign gained international support

The fight for freedom

Many people in South Africa came to think of Mandela as a symbol of the fight for freedom in their country. By 1980, the campaign to free Mandela had found worldwide support. Finally, in 1990, Mandela was released from prison by the new president of South Africa, F W de Klerk. He was 71 years old.

Free at last: Mandela celebrates his release from prison

President Mandela

In April 1994, a general election was held, and for the first time people of all races could vote. Mandela led the ANC to victory and became president of South Africa. He introduced laws to improve the quality of health, housing and education for poor South Africans.

Mandela proudly casts his vote in the 1994 election

A popular figure

In May 1999, at the age of 80, Mandela retired. He is still a very important public figure. Every year on his birthday, South Africans celebrate all the work he did to bring black and white South Africans closer together.

1990	Released from prison
1993	Mandela and de Klerk awarded Nobel Peace Prize
1989 F W de Klerk becomes president of South Africa	**1994** Elected president of South Africa
	1998 Divorces Winnie Mandela
	1999 Retires from politics

WOULD YOU BELIEVE IT?

Caroline Clare of Canada was reported to be magnetic. Knives and forks could be attached to her skin and they stayed there without any obvious help.

Fully-grown adults have five square metres of skin covering their bodies.

A baby can get hiccups before it is born.

In China in 1995, a dentist completed a three-metre-high tower made from teeth he had taken out. He built it to frighten villagers into looking after their teeth.

For 23 years, a man in Wisconsin hibernated every winter from November to Easter.

The average person swallows 295 times while eating a meal.

An old cure for whooping cough is to eat a mouse boiled in milk!

Human beings are amazing! Did you know that we have 8 million hairs on our bodies? Or that you can help get rid of a cold by eating curry? Here are some more fantastic facts about humans and their bodies.

During the day, a human body shrinks by about a centimetre. It goes back to its usual size when we lie down to sleep overnight.

The world speed record for a sneeze is 165 kilometres an hour. A sneeze can travel over 3.5 metres!

A woman who lived in London in the 18th century was so afraid of catching cold, she never washed. Instead she smeared her face and hands with lard. She lived to be 116 years old.

The tongue is the strongest muscle in the human body. It is the only muscle which is not attached at both ends.

In the 1890s, it was fashionable for women to have very small, thin waists. Some women had operations to remove their lowest ribs so they looked fashionable.

The nail on the middle finger grows fastest. The nail on the thumb grows slowest.

People can survive unknown injuries for many years. Joy Connor, an Englishwoman, had a broken neck for 45 years without knowing it.

Human babies can grow up to 1.5 centimetres in a single day.

Byte-Sized ICT

Six of the best

Favourite sports

Design a survey about attitudes to sport in your class. You could find out which sports your classmates enjoy taking part in most, which sports they enjoy watching, how often they watch sport live, how often they take exercise, and so on.

Type your questions on a word-processor. When you have collected your data, enter it into a data-handling program. This will allow you to show your results in a variety of ways. Alternatively, you could set up a database and ask each member of your class to enter their own data. When everyone has entered their data, you can view it and sort it in different ways.

Always check the data you have entered, in case any mistakes have crept in. For example, if some people say their favourite sport is soccer and some call the same game football, this will count as two categories. You will need to be eagle-eyed!

Water world

Super scuba stunts

Can you invent some spectacular stunts? Imagine you are an ambitious producer of an action-packed movie. Use a graphics program to draw some pictures of amazing stunts. Make them as hair-raising as you can! Perhaps it could be a hero trying to rescue something from underwater, or maybe a baddie escaping in a daredevil way! Make sure you add some text labels to show what's going on.

Wham-Bam Sockowski

Who's your hero?

Do you have a favourite sports star? Why not use the Internet to find out more about them? Many famous sports personalities have their own websites. Try searching by their name or sport. If they play for a team, you could look up the site of the team they play for.

Remember, if you are using a search engine always include a couple of key words to focus your search. Don't forget to use 'and' to keep your search narrow.

If you find some interesting information, print it out and use a highlighter pen to pick out three points that interest you the most. Then type them up using a word-processor, putting them in your own words.

Eureka!

Learning to be web-wise

It's great to use the Internet to find out more about a science topic that interests you, or to help you understand more about some science you've done in class. There are some really useful sites designed especially for children, that tell you more in a fun way, and some that even allow you to play games or test yourself on science topics.

Why not spend some time searching for a couple of really useful science websites that you think are worth a look? Instead of just looking at them and then leaving them, however, make sure you take a note of their website addresses to share with others and use next time you need to do some science. You may even have the facility to save the address in a 'favourites' file on your computer: then it will only be a click away.

Giving us goosebumps

What's your view?

Have you ever read a book by R L Stine? Did you love it or hate it? Did it give you goosebumps? If you have read one (or more!), why not use a word-processor to type a short review of it, including your overall opinion of *Goosebumps* books?

You could encourage a few friends who have read books by Stine to add their comments to the document. Each person could choose a different font or colour to make each entry stand out. You might even find a scary-style font or two! When everyone has finished, print the document out and see whether everyone enjoyed the books.

Would you believe it?

Body beautiful

There are some amazing facts about the human body on pages 24 and 25. Use a publishing program to present some of them as a poster about the wonders of the human body. You may even know a few more amazing facts of your own or have your own unusual party piece! Perhaps you can touch your nose with your tongue or fold your ears inside out!

To make it more fun, you could include digital photos to illustrate some of the facts. You'll probably need the help of a few friends who don't mind being photographed or who can photograph you! Get posing!

Glossary

acclaimed	admired, applauded
apartheid	apartness – the policy of keeping people of different races separated in some way
aquanaut	an underwater explorer
campaign	act in support of a particular important issue
Celts	people who lived in Britain before the Romans. When the Romans came, they retreated into Scotland, Wales and Cornwall, where their descendents still live
centenary	a 100th anniversary
combatant	someone taking part in a fight or battle
consistency	the thickness or feel of something
decades	periods of ten years
decathlon	a contest in which athletes compete for the highest total score in ten separate events
depict	show in paintings or drawings
diabetes	a disease caused when too much sugar builds up in someone's blood
enthusiastic	keen and excited
habitat	the natural home or environment of animals and plants
heptathlon	a contest in which athletes compete for the highest total score in seven separate events

hibernate	sleep through the winter
Hundred Years War	a war between England and France that lasted from 1337 until 1453
immigrant	someone who enters and settles in a country or region
lard	the fat from a pig, prepared for use in cooking
leisure	time free from work or duties
lever	a bar, supported somewhere along its length, that you use to lift or move a weight
marine biologist	a scientist who studies things that live in the sea
morals	behaviour based on what is right or good
murals	pictures that are painted on walls
privileged	a person having special advantages
revenge	getting your own back
silver jubilee	an anniversary marking 25 years of a king or queen's reign
stunt	a bold, daring, dangerous or unusual act
tucker	slang word for food, used frequently in Australia

Index